D0474407

TRAVEL LIGHT TRAVEL DARK

John Agard was born in Guyana and came to Britain in 1977. His many books include six collections from Bloodaxe, *From the Devil's Pulpit* (1997), *Weblines* (2000), *We Brits* (2006), *Alternative Anthem: Selected Poems* (2009), *Clever Backbone* (2009) and *Travel Light Travel Dark* (2013). He was awarded the Queen's Gold Medal for Poetry 2012.

He won the Casa de las Américas Prize in 1982 for *Man to Pan*, a Paul Hamlyn Award in 1997, and a Cholmondeley Award in 2004. *We Brits* was shortlisted for the 2007 Decibel Writer of the Year Award, and he has won the Guyana Prize twice, first for *From the Devil's Pulpit* and then for *Weblines*.

As a touring speaker with the Commonwealth Institute, he visited nearly 2000 schools promoting Caribbean culture and poetry, and has performed on television and around the world. In 1993 he became the first Writer in Residence at London's South Bank Centre, which published *A Stone's Throw from Embankment*, a collection written during that residency. In 1998 he was writer-in-residence for the BBC with the Windrush project, and *Bard at the Beeb*, a selection of poems written during that residency, was published by BBC Learning Support. He was writer in residence at the National Maritime Museum in Greenwich in 2007.

He is a popular children's writer whose titles include *Get Back Pimple* (Viking), *Laughter is an Egg* (Puffin), *Grandfather's Old Bruk-a-down Car* (Red Fox), *I Din Do Nuttin* (Red Fox), *Points of View with Professor Peekaboo* (Bodley Head) and *We Animals Would Like a Word with You* (Bodley Head), which won a Smarties Award. *Einstein, The Girl Who Hated Maths*, a collection inspired by mathematics, and *Hello H_2O*, a collection inspired by science, were published by Hodder Children's Books and illustrated by Satoshi Kitamura. Frances Lincoln Children's Books published his recent titles *The Young Inferno* (2008), his retelling of Dante, also illustrated by Satoshi Kitamura, which won the CLPE Poetry Award 2009, and *Goldilocks on CCTV* (2011). His anthology *Hello New* (Orchard Books, 2000) was chosen by the Poetry Society as its Children's Poetry Bookshelf Best Anthology.

He lives with the poet Grace Nichols and family in Sussex; they received the CLPE Poetry Award 2003 for their children's anthology *Under the Moon and Over the Sea* (Walker Books).

JOHN AGARD

TRAVEL LIGHT
TRAVEL DARK

BLOODAXE BOOKS

Copyright © John Agard 2013

ISBN: 978 1 85224 991 5

First published 2013 by
Bloodaxe Books Ltd,
Eastburn,
South Park,
Hexham,
Northumberland NE46 1BS.

Second impression 2015

www.bloodaxebooks.com
For further information about Bloodaxe titles
please visit our website or write to
the above address for a catalogue.

Supported by
**ARTS COUNCIL
ENGLAND**

LEGAL NOTICE

All rights reserved. No part of this book may be
reproduced, stored in a retrieval system, or
transmitted in any form, or by any means, electronic,
mechanical, photocopying, recording or otherwise,
without prior written permission from Bloodaxe Books Ltd.

Requests to publish work from this book
must be sent to Bloodaxe Books Ltd.

John Agard has asserted his right under
Section 77 of the Copyright, Designs and Patents Act 1988
to be identified as the author of this work.

Cover design: Neil Astley & Pamela Robertson-Pearce.

Printed in Great Britain by
Bell & Bain Limited, Glasgow, Scotland.

for Grace as ever
and for Michael Gilkes
my sixth-former teacher-inspirer
and for Stewart Brown
my Mabinogion–Caribbean–cricket–conspirer

In mirrored hues we have our life and being.

GOETHE

(1749-1832)

ACKNOWLEDGEMENTS

Thanks to Diana Reich for commissioning 'Sloth' for the Brighton Festival (1998) centenary celebration of the birth of Bertolt Brecht and commemorating his libretto *Seven Deadly Sins*; and thanks to Carol Ann Duffy for commissioning a war poetry supplement for the *Guardian* (2009) where 'In Times of Peace' first appeared; and a wedding vows poetry supplement (2011), also for the *Guardian*, where 'Nuptials' first appeared.

'The Price of Sleep' first appeared in *Shoot Me With Flowers* (1972), a slim self-published first collection in Guyana. 'Child Waiting' first appeared in *Mangoes & Bullets* (Pluto Press, 1985). with thanks to Peter Ayrton. 'Prospero Caliban Cricket' first appeared in *New Writing 2*, ed. Malcolm Bradbury and Andrew Motion (Minerva, 1993). 'Give the Ball to the Poet' first appeared in *Chapman*. 'For a Piano Lost in Lewes Flood: October 2000' first appeared in *Poetry South* (ed. John Davies) and *The Frogmore Papers* (ed. Jeremy Page), two Sussex-based publications. 'Remember the ship' first appeared in *Bard at The Beeb* (1998), poems written as BBC poet-in-residence and published by BBC Learning Support with thanks to Jeffrey Morris and Steve Pollock. 'Theseus Writes Home from the Barbican', commissioned by Gillian Barker, first appeared in a Barbican brochure (2007) celebrating their 25th anniversary.

Early versions of 'Atlantic Libation', 'What Ails the King?', 'Old Father Thames' and 'The Letter-writing Ghost of Ignatius Sancho' were written during a writer's residency at the National Maritime Museum and first appeared on their website. My thanks to Indie Chowrudri who initiated the residency and to Flora Gordon for their support during the residency.

Thanks to Mark Hewitt for reading the *Colour Poems* over a pint of Guinness and for his helpful suggestion.

Thanks to Sarah Lawrence for introducing me to the Goliard tradition by passing on her copy of *The Goliard Poets* (translated by George F. Whicher and published by New Directions, 1949) and sowing the seed for a new spin on one of the tavern songs. This version of 'The Wine and Water Debate' was first performed at the United Emirates Literature Festival in Dubai, 2011.

CONTENTS

COLOUR POEMS

*

There's a poem dressed in black
standing beside your sleep. Night's troubadour.
The poem dressed in black retraces tracks
to rediscover voices lost in history's footnotes.
They say the poem dressed in black
lets the raven's quill speak for the unheard
and will take your charity and feed it to the birds.

*

There's a poem dressed in white
waving the dove of a flag for the fallen
when peace becomes a forgotten language.
It shimmers in the halo of the blank page.
They say the poem dressed in white
takes on the role of the angelic host
for those who trust in the footprints of ghosts.

*

There's a poem dressed in grey
contemplating a handful of cinders.
It lends an ear to architect and arsonist.
Makes itself at home in a house of ashes.
They say the poem dressed in grey
wears its heart on a sleeve of fog for a joke
and dwells in the folds of a moth's twilight cloak.

*

There's a poem dressed in red
announcing its fire on your flesh.
Feel its wayward tongue possess you
in places you liked to think were secret.
They say the poem dressed in red
makes an art of bleeding slowly –
your very veins its new-found Calvary.

*

There's a poem dressed in yellow
plucking stars from memory's dark chambers.
They say the poem dressed in yellow
is not all happy ribbons round old oak trees.
It knows the flesh of the sun also bleeds
and wears the face of spring as a second skin.
Under a sunflower's gold it shelters death's grin.

*

There's a poem dressed in green
somersaulting like a child on the grass.
No use pointing to the sign KEEP OFF THE GRASS
when blades of innocence invite abandon.
They say the poem dressed in green
thrives on a single leaf's transfiguration.
One leaf will do to build a paradise on.

*

There's a poem dressed in brown
filling your ears with a chorus of dead leaves,
while under your feet the worms prepare their sermon:
simply that all things must come to pass,
civilisations crumble in the quiet of the hourglass.
They say the poem dressed in brown
puts aside such thoughts to bask in bread's reflection.

*

There's a poem dressed in purple
wandering amidst a crowd of mourners.
It keeps the company of covered mirrors
and photos preserved in memory's shroud.

They say the poem dressed in purple
talks to lavender in an empty bed
and reserves a royal seat for the dead.

*

There's a poem dressed in blue
walking on water through furrows of faith.
A believer in miracles and the horizon's eye.
A collaborator with sea and sky.

They say the poem dressed in blue
invites all into its looking-glass abyss –
forever infinity's accomplice.

*

There's a poem dressed in pink
wrapping your nightmares in candy floss.
It has a way of shocking sweetly.
All you who dream in colour, be warned.
They say the poem dressed in pink
begins by tinting your eyelids rosy,
all the better to set your demons free.

*

There's a poem dressed in orange
grinning at itself in a pumpkin mirror
when October puts on its Halloween robe.
They say the poem dressed in orange
comes to take a humble place at your table,
yet from its navel radiates a god-glow.
Who invited this Buddha to squat in your fruit bowl?

WATER MUSIC

Water Music of a Different Kind

(after Handel's)

1

Water/   maker of distance from old born ground

Water/

     iron fist in billowing gloves

Water/   burial shroud for the drowned ones
     names lost to a sleep of salt

Water/   of ocean never seen before
where are the lullabyes and praise songs
in your daylong nightlong roar?

Water
whale-path
ship-path
flying-fish path
but no homecoming door.

2

Here beside the Thames
away from the clatter of the chains
heaven is an open barge
of Handel's upward flowing strains
that would so impress King George
two encores if you please
join their air to July's breeze.

Here beside the Thames
time is measured in curtseys
money counted in guineas

22

and the moans of the bassoon
a far cry from the hell
of a crowded barracoon
where there's no room for Handel.

Here beside the Thames
the weather has been kind.
No canefields shedding flames.
It's minuet time.
Lefthand turn.
Righthand turn.
No sunup to sundown.
Chop and burn.
Chop and burn.
No uprising to upset
a measured minuet

Not yet.

3

Water music of a different kind.
No sweet F-major suite
releasing golden crystals
to a river's ear.
But a dumbing middle passage bell
tolling a tale of shackled feet.
Footsteps without fanfare.

Water music of a different kind.
Water music of Atlantic winds and strings.
Water music of a speechless throat
far removed from ruffles and lace.
No Handel from open boat
drifting at a summer's pace
towards the halls of Chelsea.

Water music of a different kind.
Water music of the muzzled tongue.
Water music of a green darkness
that answers to the name of ocean.
And not one hut or shrine
to bless the emptiness
of a nowhere horizon.

Water music of a cursed crossing.
Water music of a navel string
once wrapped in Africa's ground
now bound to a ship's chamber-hold.
Water music of a splintered gourd
waiting to be tolled.
Which mouth will toll its story?

4

If you could talk, sweet Thames,
of bleeding continents
still shackled to your sub-text

what words would you resurrect
to mark the unsung lives
in your rippling register?

What words, sweet Thames,
to catalogue the shadows that stalk
your murky archives

the demons under your swans

the bouquet of heads piked
on your iconic bridge
to adorn a royal thirst

or how your soft corridors
blessed a knighted breed
to fill empire's purse?

Yet when a summer's evening comes
to illuminate your script,
one bridge will do to cast a spell

and lull to sleep history's traffic
in the arms of sublime Handel.

5

Say your piece
conch-shell
mouthpiece
of sea and wind

talk your talk
talking drum
spread your goatskin
gospel

feature this
Atlantic abyss
with a face
of syllables

kindle this void
with the flame
of living breath.
Memory's candle –

for all who leapt
with their names
into the gaping
shelving of the sea.

6

Glass beads ask no questions
firearms point no finger
when pieces of the Indies
outweigh the curse
of what's been called
'beneficial commerce'.

And while Handel's serenade
soars above transatlantic trade
there are signs of revelation
in the witness of rivers –
the rise and fall of conscience
from water's haunting chambers.

7

Beware beware
the Bight of Benin.
Few come out
though many go in.

How far how far
to old Calabar
where human bounty
is enterprise.

Not far not far
the Thames replies.
As far as the crow
of Europe flies.

Just a slaver's throw
from a Chelsea ball
to the upper arm
of the Senegal.

Is that the blood
of the Gambia
flowing under
a Thames aria?

8

Rivers of conscience
Rivers of conscience
Which way to the source
of redemption's dance?

Here beside the Thames
where the hornpipes thrill
wheel your partner round
wheel your partner round?

Or on those plantations
where sugar sweetly kills
and black bodies learn
to master the quadrille?

Lefthand turn.
            Righthand turn.
Canefield burn.
            Big house burn.

Rivers of conscience
Rivers of conscience
Which way to the source
of redemption's dance?

9

Water music of the womb's first fountain
Water music of the eyes' running stream

Water music of the parched tongue greeting rain
Water music of the blood's common spring

Water music of heart opening its door
Water music of mind widening its shore

Water music of a new beginning.
Human crossing into human crossing.

CROSSINGS

Atlantic Libation

1

What light can your green darkness, Atlantic,
shed on a traffic that has scarred your waters?
Say something, Atlantic.
In your unending ebb and flow
do you spare a minute's silence
for the tongues shrouded in your limbo?
What of the souls who entered your liquid door?

Since water, according to the native Indians,
is not without feeling,
and rings a bell of healing in any language,
in the crescendo of your tides, Atlantic,
do you sound a solitary note
for the oblivion of your blighted passage
where names have lost their meaning?

Speak, Atlantic.

Or are you history's silent accomplice?

2

If I Atlantic were to shame
my winds into a minute's silence
I would demand of the conch shell
a breathless elegy
for all the unmourned
gathered in my memory
and that my tides salute their loss.

Alas, even I Atlantic
with my Middle Passage baggage
must find in my limbo some fetish of hope
to lay room for horizons.
Some silver lining in my ebb and flow.
Some olive leaf in my salty depths
pointing towards unshackled footsteps.

For an ocean knows the meaning of freedom
as water knows the reason for a bridge.
Yet how can I Atlantic watch my waters
steeped in cursed crossings
become a cross for continents to bear
and not break my silent pledge?
What can I bring to history's sacrificial altar

but the salt of myself sprinkled in libation
to flavour the course of new bloodstreams –
I Atlantic weaving dreams from my tainted cloth
to embody the fabric of a future...

Columbus Discovers Himself

Sailing interior seas is a risky enterprise.

Who knows what Other dwells
under the skin's uncharted skies?

What manner of fauna and flora
will the blood's Sargasso deliver?

The brain's treacherous horizon ahoy.
The tierra incognita of self-discovery.

O mapless mariner lost in his inner Indies.

Carib She-Baby

Humming bird eyes
and palmtree hair
beware beware
the Carib She-Baby
she make history weak
at the knees
when she move
she move like a breeze
cause wind cradle she
in the antilles
rock she windward
rock she leeward

Humming bird eyes
and palmtree hair
watch for the Carib She-Baby
deep wandering
behind she coral grin
she leap over water
before she learn to creep
when she whisper she whisper
she bone turn flute
when she scream she scream
she tremble tree root
cause hurricane
she grandmother
and legend the name
of she race
                    Carib She-Baby-o
                    Carib She-Baby-o
                    Carib She-Baby-o

River Called Rum

Light golden brown
dark reflective brown

sometimes sunhot white
changing colour with the light

this river called Rum
does flow steady-steady

towards the red sea
of your blood

and flood
the dam of your brains

winding past treacherous
rocks of ice

to entice
many a galleon

to a watery end
and many a skull and crossbone

was known to perish
for a gallon of this liquid gold

not to mention the ancestral limb
scattered like a broken fetish.

Pour a glass of this river
and lift history to your lips.

Sugar Cane's Saga

Blessed by centuries' sun and rain
I'll spill the saga of my nectar
whose Indus flowed inside of me
even as I rustled in a Persian breeze
and waved my tassels in Egypt's furrows.
And who should choose me for a bow
who but Kama, the love-god –
honeybees his string
flower tips his arrows
and I Sugar Cane his ready bow.
With such a trinity
joining forces in the name of love,
how can heart and limb not surrender
to the flames of my sweetness?
Yet, as the Chinese say, don't expect
Sugar Cane to be sweet at both ends.
And bitter was yet to come, my friend.

No sea was too far-flung to hear my name.
The Red Sea. The Black Sea. The Mediterranean.
I added my shadow to the olive and the fig
and rejoiced with sycamore in the slopes of Jericho,
for had I not sweetened Arabia's caravans?
My taste was paradise on a caliph's tongue.
In the desert of a mouth my name flowed
like the honey of holy utterance:
Al-zucar. Al-zucar. Al-zucar.

And so I spilled myself into streams of language.
Yuh can't suck cane and whistle –
a reminder from the Caribbean proverb.
Far and wide tastebud bells rang my homage.

In Madeira where that mariner
put my growing to the test
I usurped the throne of wheat.
In Spain I invaded the quince's meat.
In England I blackened a fair queen's teeth.
How Europe's teacups hungered for my blessing.

Name me a city: Venice. London. Paris. Amsterdam.
My crystals pierced their jellies and their jams
I made their potions friendlier to swallow.
I was the miracle in their cocoa.
My jointed stem joined the fates of continents.
I flourished in the wake of caravels
and my white gold would gather poor souls
cast to plantations from Atlantic's hell.
O deep in my spine I still hear Africa's heartbeat
and begin to taste the bitter in my sweet
even as in my knotted juices
I still spill India's indentured bruises.

Now while tourists revel
in my amniotic rum
I Sugar Cane stand
pointing to history's crossroads
my double-edged tongue
translating the wind
my sweet finger stirring
the cup of conscience
as once the embers of myself
signalled harvest as well as uprising.

What Ails the King?

He who drinks a tumbler of London water has literally in his stomach more animated beings than there are men and women and children on the face of the earth.

REVEREND SYDNEY SMITH 1771-1845

A tumbler of London water
A tumbler of London water
And make that sparkling hybrid.
A King can't have enough of this multi-fluid.

I want to feel as Druid as oak
as Roman as Severus, that Libyan bloke,
as pagan-powered as up-in-arms Boadicea
as lettered as that black Victorian Sancho.

O water from the well of hidden histories
as angel-fruitful as Blake's Peckham Rye tree
as Sabbath-lit as a Jewish window
as spice-warm as a Huguenot-haunted curry house.

I want to salaam as shalom
and be dragon-driven as Chinatown
where old grey Thames meets the Yellow River
and the little bardic people of the Irish Sea.

My kingdom, I say, my sceptered kingdom
for a tumbler of London H_2O.
Let animated beings invade my being.
Let a King imbibe the globe in one swallow.

Slip of a Riddle

Fruit of a tree
that's a plant to purists

lacking blood and bone
yet a fleshly digit

a yellow reminder
of Miss Baker in Paris

a tropical finger
pointing to republics

now thinly moon-sliced
for your Weetabix

now a pick-me-up
for Wimbledon's peckish

now a mindless missile
hurled at a football pitch.

Yet it brought a smile –
that day in 1946

when it made an exotic
comeback after the Blitz

and a London lord mayor
was at the docks to greet it

and little postwar mouths
had lessons in how to eat it.

Step on its skin
at your own risk.

And even as you slip –
Salute the banana.

Some Things Never Change

What do you do when faces from foreign lands
make your island their home ground?
You wake to find your fields and woods
berserk with bearded Scandinavians.

Have they crossed the sea-road in their longships
to take away our Saxon jobs
and fill our women's ears
with nerve-tingling Norse gutturals?

Can our better halves resist one
with a name like Jobjörn the horse-bear,
Olaf the stout, Thorkell the tall?
Are they as stallion in the sack as they sound?

Mind you, they all look alike,
this northman breed of brawn whose bards
match ours for the gift of glee.
This much we have in common.

Now take old Snorsson, my ale-mate.
True, his Dane blood makes him one of them.
But he's different, more like one of us.
I love the bastard to the bone.

Many a night we drowned our differences
and made the air merry with brawl and banter.
Once you get to know them, Vikings aren't a bad lot.
Easier to fathom than the Welsh or Scot.

As for my daughter hitching
her pagan limbs to some longship foreigner,
over my dead body! But who am I
to stop the tide of Thor the thunderer?

Prospero Caliban Cricket

(for C.L.R. James)

Prosper batting
Caliban bowling
and is cricket is cricket in yuh ricketics
but from far it look like politics.

Caliban running up
from beyond de boundary
because he come
from beyond de boundary
if you know yuh history.

Prospero standing
bat and pad
thinking Caliban is a mere lad
from a new-world archipelago
and new to the game.

But not taking chances
Prospero invoking de name
of W.G. Grace
to preserve him
from a bouncer to the face.

Caliban if he want
could invoke duppy jumbie
zemi baccoo all kinda ting,
but instead he relying
just pon pace and swing.

Caliban arcing de ball
like an unpredictable whip
Prospero foot like it chain to de ground.
Before he could mek a move
de ball gone thru to de slip.

And de way de crowd rocking
you would think dey crossing de Atlantic.

Is cricket is cricket in yuh ricketics
but from far it look like politics.
Prospero remembering
how Caliban used to call him master.
Now Caliban agitating de ball faster
and de crowd shouting Power.

Caliban remembering
how Prospero used to call him knave and serf.
Now Caliban striding de cricket turf
like he breathing a nation,
and de ball swinging it own way
like it hear bout self-determination.

Is cricket is cricket in yuh ricketics
but from far it look like politics.
Prospero wishing
Shakespeare was de umpire,
Caliban see a red ball
and he see fire
rising with glorious uncertainty.
Prospero front pad forward with diplomacy

Is cricket is cricket in yuh ricketics
but from far it look like politics.
Prospero invoking
de god of snow
wishing a shower of flakes
would stop all play,
but de sky so bright with carib glow
you can't even appeal for light
much less ask for snow.

Is cricket is cricket in yuh ricketics
but from far it look like politics.

Give the Ball to the Poet

(for Angus Calder)

If is true de poet
does commune with nature,
then de fast bowler (don't forget)
does talk to de wind.
So rub a poem on yuh flannel,
rub till de poem red as hell.
About time de poet
have a little spell.

Is all right when words sing
in lyrical flight,
but when dey also have grit
and double bite,
de literary boys dem call it
ambiguity of meaning.
I rather call it double entendre swing
of a Michael Holding.

Is strictly hurricane whispering
in a six-ball sonnet.
Now and then drop one short
like a flick-of-the-wrist haiku.
Bounce a home truth or two
and force a conscience
to go for a stroke.

You might think I aiming joke
at the laws of the canon,
if I say poetry is de motion
of three wrecked stumps
re-collected in tranquillity.

But is no laughing matter
when a poet feeling on de boundary,
and a crowd hungry for blood
start to shout a prophecy:
Give the ball to the poet.

Tupaia Sketches

(for Jan Carew, global-eye piai-man)

Tupaia was the Tahitian who as navigator and translator sailed with Captain Cook on the Endeavour *in 1769. Intrigued by European science, he also did watercolours which have been stored at the British Library and which capture the earliest encounter between Europeans and the indigenous Maoris and Aborigines.*

Sun   my day-compass
moon and stars   my night-compass
wind and clouds   my direction-giver
cry of bird   my landfall-messenger
the very veins of water   my wrinkled map
old as the pearls   of Taha'a

But what ghosts of far away water
have made their god-house in this captain's heart
that nothing dims his hunger for horizons
and naming islands after his own tongue?

Ah Raiatea of the sky's soft light
my born-ground where feathers speak louder than words
far from the shadows of your tamanu trees
Tupaia has become Cook's tongue and gesture.

This memory I will put down
on white man's paper for my tapa cloth.
Out of Europe's paintbox –
Tupaia the Chief Mourner
will speak in waters of colour.
Sketch that first exchange of gifts –
a handkerchief for a crayfish –
Aotearoa, land of the long white cloud,
fading into New Zealand on a stranger's lips –
my pencil my witness.

We the Forgotten Names.

You say the forgotten names are no more
you say the forgotten names are gone.

But we the forgotten names say to you
We are not footprints on a lost shore

We still follow in canoes of spirit
wherever our children endure horizons

taking directions from nature's chart
as when naked bark first married water –

these navigators who worship in feathers.
The long-tailed cuckoo their longitude

the stars their gleaming compass
a hint of seaweed their Land Ahoy.

And how their tongues took joy
in the dreaming of new homecomings

for land was not a conqueror's glass
reflecting shadows of dominion.

We the forgotten names grew wings
not from the crests of fading monarchs

but from the crown of bird, tree, stone.
We the forgotten names lost in history's log

rewrite ourselves on a page of bone –
our buried syllables surface from the sea's ink.

I Am the Oak That Became a Ship

Hearts of oak our ships
Hearts of oak our men,
We always are ready, steady boys, steady,
To charge and conquer again and again.

Anthem of British Navy: REVEREND RYLANCE 1809

Of my flesh and bone
was made Europe's first boat
to enter a world
they would call New –
a world away from acorns
and winter's white hold.
I helped extend Europe's arm
as those Vikings well knew
and Nelson too.

Anchored to woodland
and forest-bed
I saw myself felled –
my limbs ship-shaped
for water's swell –
my arms un-draped –
no glimmer of squirrel –
my tarred veins sea-ready.
The tide calling out my name.

I Oak – a fallen god
finding a new way to leap.
And so my ribs set sail
my cleft skin braved the deep –
mistletoe, a forgotten touch.
My now dolphin body
brought horizons closer
till the globe was a purse
and conscience fell to sleep.

Charon on Thames

There he goes ferrying souls across the Thames.
Ferryman Charon in tweed and cloth cap
To the Underworld he's Lord Charon, old chap.

His credentials are Hades-approved.
Rumour has it he's a refugee Greek.
But his accent is estuary – when he does speak.

Lord Charon, old chap, has the knowledge.
He knows the scenic route to eternity
via the waters of your inner city.

Call him the afterlife's middle man.
A dealer in shades this side of heaven.
Mixes the forgivers with the forgiven.

Believers, disbelievers, all,
gather on your passing at Embankment pier
where the ferryman awaits without fanfare.

The crossing will set you back one coin.
It's value for small change in the mouth of the dead.
You can pay by euro or the Queen's silver head.

With a brolly for a pole, chop-chop,
he ferries souls of Brits and gives them their due.
Even in death they keep their place in a queue.

Ah Thames, ah Styx, ah Acheron.
How the anthems of the gone cry as one.
The common tongue no less than Agamemnon's.

Old Father Thames

Old Father Thames
of the flowing patriarchal locks
See how the Ganges still breathes

in your West India docks.
See how the Nile's distant kiss
still finds the cheeks of your metropolis

Old Father Thames
Empire's wrinkles etch your tide.
About time you reclaimed your feminine side.

Try laying down your trident, old chap.
Take the weight of anchors and maps
from off your monumental head.

Have a good squat, old Father Thames.
Squat on your dark silted bed
till birth screams of changing winds

turn you midwife to a new beginning.

Theseus Writes Home from the Barbican

I who had dared the challenging pathways of Crete
kept a lookout for beech trees in Beech Street
and hoped for signs of silk in Silk Street.
Arrows pointing were my Ariadne's thread
yet I found myself going back on myself
lost among the ever-rising gestures of concrete
while my footsteps stayed faithful to my quest.
I called on Hecate, goddess of the crossroads,
she who with one glance embraces all directions,
to guide me to the place they call the Barbican.
But it was a traffic warden who pointed the path:
'You can't miss it. It's staring you in the face, mate.'
There before me stood a many-towered estate
with potted sentinels of cascading ivy
draping their green trail round grey balconies.
And in the coolness of a springtime sun
fountains gushed their water-lipped orations.
And all this in a world of concrete and glass
that led me deeper into a maze of what's called the Arts.
Yes, the Minotaur's hideout was a piece of cake
compared to this labyrinth of the mind's making,
this bull-leaping arena for imagination's play
where Goya's ghosts meet a Japanese Coriolanus.
How I longed for Ariadne's winding compass
in this maze that amazes Theseus.
Now writing these few lines by the Waterside Café
I ponder a place where they say bombs once fell
and how dust has surrendered to a lone laurel.

Enlightenment

Before Newton's boyhood pebble
revealed to him its inward lesson
of truth's undiscovered ocean –
some dreaming soul branded savage
once stood on some uncharted shore
and heard the voice of thunder in a stone.

Meeting of Mirrors

In the mirror
of mariners
blessed by Church and Sovereign

the original islanders
are dusky others
steeped in original sin

In the mirror
of mariners
blessed by a shaman's bone

old world newcomers
are ghost-skinned others
bearing new thunder in their arms

such meeting of mirrors
such scattering of splinters

Congo to Llandudno

In 1892 the Welsh Baptist missionary, William Hughes, returned from Africa to Llandudno pier with two Congolese boys to initiate his Congo House project which was to become the African Training Institute (1893-1912) in Colwyn Bay, north Wales. The aim was to recruit African students and have them trained in a craft and in Christian values before they went back to their native lands as self-supporting missionaries. Gravestones tell a tale of Congolese buried in Colwyn cemetery.

1

How many miles to Llandudno?
How far that place from Congo?

As far as ship
from the hut that witnessed your first steps
As far as sheep
from the buffalo that roams your forest

And though ship be sound
and sail be bright
you'll not be there
by candlelight

How many miles to Llandudno?
How far that place from Congo?

2

A missionary's north Wales dream your leap of faith
into a world as far as esobe grass from slate –
you who came with names like Nkanza and Kinkasa.

At chapel you were a pious talking point.
Pastor Hughes' African cherubs in white neckties.
You would raise Revelation to Welsh skies

and spill the Psalms from memory's valley.
How quaint in your mouths King Arthur's banned tongue
as if dipped in waters of the Mabinogion.

And while you feared no evil from Colwyn Bay's sands
John Bull's tabloid of the day would warn no good
can come of walks with local lasses in the woods.

3

How many miles to Congo?
How far that place from Llandudno?

As far as antelope's leap
from a pastor's last breath in a Colwyn workhouse
As far as born-laughing-Mwindo's floating drum
from the Amens of Congo's sons under Welsh ground

Yet as close as a hymn
that leaves its mouthprint in a valley
as close as the chapel bell
that tolls a litany of Sundays
as close as the dark gene
still singing from the blood's uncharted gospel.

Lashkar Odyssey

Sailors who were from the East Indies and who worked on British ships came to be known as Lashkars, from the Urdu, Persian and Arabic, meaning army. The word was also used of soldiers of East Indian origin in the British army.

1

By the waters of the Thames we sat down
and there we remembered Mother Ganga.
How her waters brought blessings to a bowl
and turned a body to a benediction.

Some of us spoke tongues dipped in ancient Vedas
some of us spoke tongues echoing the Koran.
Simple to call us those dark-skinned sailors
simpler to call us strangers in a strange land.

O the Bay of Bengal was going going gone
as history's hammer pointed towards London.
Shall we hang our sitars from weeping willows
and sing an eastern song to the bells of Bow?

Tread softly, stranger, through these built-up dockyards.
In the wind there is a word for us: Lashkar.

2

Horizons parted company with the Ganges.
Anchors weighed heavy in the waters of our dreams
till the cobra of the Thames unwound its dance
and hope was Hanuman's hands spanning the distance.

Where was the lotus in this river's imperial mud?
Where were the garlands waiting at those docks?
And if our days at sea signalled things to come,
expect grey hours keeping time by empire's clocks.

From China. From Burma. From Africa. The Punjab.
All turned towards the call of a single flag.
Red sashed, white trousered, dark blue tuniced.
All rolled into an ocean's citizenship.

Adrift on London's streets, we scattered Bengal's stars
to seed a foreign sky. Now home. Now close. Now far.

The Letter-writing Ghost of Ignatius Sancho

*Born on a slave ship, Ignatius Sancho (1729-1780) was given the name
by his first patrons, three Greenwich sisters, after Don Quixote's squire,
Sancho. He later joined the household of the Duke of Montagu as a valet
and his letters, published two years after his death, made him the first
African man of letters in 18th-century Britain.*

Ah, dear Sir, how pleasant to partake alfresco
at a café called *The Honest Sausage*
and simply be Ignatius Sancho,
surveying Greenwich Park with Moorish visage.
I dare say the Duke himself, old Montagu,
would relish an honest sausage on the menu.
Alas, I see the old house, like the good Duke, gone.
And skateboards have taken the place of swans,
while little Brits with diasporas in their skin
learn to occupy the centre and the margin.
But I shall not line my tongue in easy rage.
Not when my mouth is filled with an honest sausage.

Mrs Sancho, my treasured best half, would deem
an honest sausage worthy of her esteem,
and approve my resting my gout-ridden feet
upon on this hill where Empire's feasting elite
once overlooked their remote middle passage
like pheasants skewered in their own plumage.
Pardon me for not mincing my sentiments,
which, like this sausage, are honestly meant.
Yet when history drops its heavy anchors,
I say let us give thanks for honest bangers.
So heartily I munch while I sit and muse
on the Atlantic coming home to roost.

Enough said. And so with belly exceeding Falstaff,
I must perforce finish before my pen has half
disgorged my heart. Mrs Sancho (bless her) is amused
that my untutored letters are now scholarly perused.

Your devoted
Ignatius Sancho

Remember the ship

As citizen
of the English tongue

I say remember
the ship
in citizenship

for language
is the baggage
we bring –

a weight
of words to ground
and give us wing –

as millennial waters
beckon wide

and love's anchor
waiting to be cast

will the ghost of race
become the albatross
we shoot at our cost?

I'm here to navigate –
not flagellate
with a whip of the past

for is not each member
of the human race
a ship on two legs

charting life's tidal
rise and fall

as the ship
of the sun
unloads its light

and the ship
of night
its cargo of stars

again I say remember
the ship
in citizenship

and diversity
shall sound its trumpet
outside the bigot's wall

and citizenship shall be
a call
to kinship

that knows
no boundary
of skin

and the heart
offer its wide harbours
for Europe's new voyage

to begin

THE DEBATE OF WINE AND WATER

The Debate of Wine and Water

(for Sarah Lawrence, version of a Latin drinking song from the Carmina Burana*)*

When some cursed hand conspires
to mix water with wine's fire,
   then the wine glass gets pissed off.
The two just can't be intertwined.
What! Wed water to Bacchus' vine?
   Would you marry wheat to chaff?

So one day, as Water drew close,
Wine screamed: 'How dare you! You gross
   liquid! I say keep your distance.
Buzz off! Sling your hook! On your bike!
By your kind I won't be spiked!
   Don't pollute my radiance.

'Water, you lowest of the low,
a foaming snake among shadows.
   Holes and cracks are where you belong.
Above ground, you're a foot's nightmare.
Slush and puddles everywhere.
   Then bloody mud before long.

'Guzzling water, can sure as hell,
make a well man feel unwell
   His insides lose their bearings.
Turbulent wind ruffles his guts
with groans confined in water's flux.
   No, Wine's far more endearing.

'Since rebel wind must be released,
through any exit it will ease
   a sudden blast of belch or fart.
And while the guts return to calm,
the atmosphere sounds an alarm
   of smells that pierce like a dart.'

Water, appalled, pointed blame:
'You, Wine, lead a life of shame.
    You're the root of iniquity.
Those who indulge in your poison
lose all their virtue and reason.
    Admit hangovers aren't pretty.

'You loosen the tongue with verbiage,
you deceive with Dutch courage.
    And whoever follows your path
staggers home a wreck, wasted –
to find their doorkey relocated.
    Nothing to do but sleep it off.

'Who do you count as bedfellows,
if not slobs, bingers and winos?
    Dwellers all in the house of booze.
Whatever their gender or shape,
they'll live and die by the grape.
    Such is the company you choose.

'Wine, you're a bottle of bother.
No wonder you're stored in cellars.
    A dungeon is where you should be.
Look at you! All corked and bound!
While I, Water, embrace the ground
    and take all earth for liberty.

'To the parched, the dehydrated,
am I not venerated?
    Who quenches better than Water?
By my drops, a sinner baptised
might yet discover Paradise –
    redeemed by the ever-after.'

Wine grinned: 'Water, say no more.
I've heard that argument before.
    And you talk like a true bigot.
Don't your very tides that guide ships
make wrecks of them? Storm-whipped.
    Looks like I've put you on the spot.

'Your speech smacks of doublespeak.
Your self-praise has sprung a leak.
    Water, you talk with forked tongue.
See how your heartless ebb and flow
makes a sailor's wife a widow.
    You get high on that small word: drown.

'Whereas I, in my godly status,
hang out with the likes of Bacchus.
    In my nectar, hearts find solace.
And was it your colour or mine
that made Canaan's miracle divine?
    How I sparkle the buds of taste.

'In the depths of my tipple,
the speechless speak in oracles.
    Fact and fiction become joined.
Those without wings grow sudden wings.
I make the tone-deaf want to sing
    and the awkward loosen their loins.

'Water, you're a cold task-master.
In your soft gloves lurks disaster.
    Water, have you no conscience?
Through me, a sloshed tongue bares all.
I turn silence to carnival
    and strangers ignite acquaintance.

'Matured, I am of vintage breed.
I encourage flesh to yield.
    I inflame the secret zones.
If only water were imbibed,
Man would be an endangered tribe.
    Not multiply by flesh and bone.'

Water replied: 'Don't make me laugh.
Have you heard of the pancreas?
    In that case, I'll fill you in.
When that fails, my friend, you've had it.
Your mortal coil meets its exit,
    for the fruit of your vine is sin.

'Wine, let me give it you straight.
Your nectar is degenerate.
    Idleness poured by decanters
gives rise to unruly banter.
By my rains, the plants say yes to green
    The flowers open into being.

Then Wine stood up all rosy-cheeked
and said: 'You're a fine one to preach.
    Disrobe your priestly clothing.
You who scatter homes to floods,
making zero of neighbourhoods.
    Do you take count of suffering?

Hearing these words, Water broke down.
Ah blessed tears. Benediction
    swimming in hometruths that were harsh.
'What do you say to that?' said Wine.
Water just said: 'Aren't tears divine?'
    and pointed Wine to withered grass.

A Hoodie in the Hood

There's a hoodie
in the hood
and it looks like a monk
acting kinda dodgy

sounds like he's swearing
in latin
and what's that he's waving?
A crucifix or a dagger?

There's a hoodie
in the hood
and it looks like a monk
with a suspicious swagger

should we ring for the police
or get down on our knees?

Jimi Hendrix and Handel Under One Roof

Hendrix moved in to 23 Brook Street, Mayfair, with his English girlfriend Kathy Etchingham in 1968. More than two centuries earlier in 1723 Handel had moved to 25 Brook Street. The two houses have since merged into one as the Handel House Museum with two heritage plaques commemorating both the composer of Messiah and the rock guitarist who lived there.

Strange how the centuries evaporate
when transatlantic ghosts become housemates
and summer 1723 puts on the swinging sixties.

Hendrix on guitar. Handel on harpsichord.
Spread the word, music lovers, spread the word.
It's the hottest gig this side of the afterlife.

One sports a powdered wig, one a western hat.
London's Mayfair heart is where the action's at.
Follow the riffs and quavers and you can't miss it.

Neighbours swore they've seen on a midsummer's rave
miniskirted sopranos tiptoeing the Georgian staircase
and they know they weren't hallucinating.

Once in the attic a guitar erupted into fire
while the study below was belting out Messiah.
O that Brook Street terrace with the two blue plaques.

Rumour has it a pair of ghosts, one white one black,
would flutter over chords and choral counterpoint.
Sometimes they'd share a hug, sometimes a joint.

But you know how gossip multiplies the truth.
Mostly H & H spoke of hippy rugs and lost love days
when childhood's oratorios bloomed in a purple haze.

Narcissus at the Flea Market

Thought I'd have a rummage, you never know.
One man's thrash is another man's treasure
and all that. Out of attics and sheds come objects
of desire, especially ones with surfaces that reflect
my own self-sparkling. That's why I have little time
for rugs and carpets. Fine for stepping on.
But they never return my radiant reflection.
The same goes for old books whose covers,
however classic, are no use for viewing one's image.
Might as well be staring into a brick.
But mirrors, ah mirrors, now you're talking my language.

Over the years I've seen myself in the oval,
in the round, scalloped, pebbled, full-length pedestalled,
down to my own handheld silvered darling.
Of course, I'd already done pools, puddles, lakes, rivers,
before graduating to mirrors and shop windows.
So imagine my joy, among a random galaxy of junk,
to encounter my familiar features in a bathroom tile,
an art deco coffee table, not to mention forgotten vinyl.
I like to call it my flea market epiphany.
Now every time I gaze into those round black discs,
I see the planet of my face beckoning me to me.

Nuptials

River, be their teacher,
that together they may turn
their future highs and lows
into one hopeful flow

Two opposite shores
feeding from a single source.

Mountain, be their milestone,
that hand in hand they rise above
familiarity's worn tracks
into horizons of their own

Two separate footpaths
dreaming of a common peak.

Birdsong, be their mantra,
that down the frail aisles of their days,
their twilight hearts twitter morning
and their dreams prove branch enough.

Riffs for a Sun-woman

(for Grace)

1

Winter rain riffs
on Sussex roof of slate

take her back
to tropical bursts

making maracas
of zinc sheet roof

a percussion
as corrugated

as memory itself
twinning continents

under her daydreaming duvet.

2

When England's sky denies her
the sun's full-blooded lantern
she must find other ways to burn

so turning inwards for heatwaves
that are kinder to sensitive skin
she turns the sun's yang into yin

and for want of hibiscus bliss
makes space for her private rays
where old tongues find new axis.

3

Oceanic as her below
sea-level Georgetown coastland
cradled by Atlantic's hand

Oceanic as the calaloo soup
tentacled with blueback crabs
her mother's spoon still paddles

Oceanic as that memory
of water's heavensent miracle
when a windfall of sunfish brought

breathing silver to a yard
and small hands went out to gather
a gospel translated into fins.

Child Waiting

(for Lesley)

Little head
at the window
in childeyed wonder

the ceasless come and go
of mighty traffic
must be moving magic
to your unblinking gaze

yet how patient
are eyes looking for one
named mummy
in a rumble of wheels.

The Price of Sleep

(for Yansan)

At two minutes past six
you screamed your wombsong coming
into a new world of shape and sound

what brings you to these shores
what dreams lie curled in your feathersoft fist
she who mothered you can never tell

but like the flower that grows
not knowing which wind will uncomb its bloom
so must you little one

so sleep well and dream your dream
before the price of sleep becomes too dear.

In the Cave of Her Mouth

(for Kalera)

It's raining vowels on her tongue
and consonants long burst
from the sky of her throat
rejoin familiar ears to the splendour
of speech newly found.

What mana of syllables fall now
to make joyous our listening?
MAMA. DADA. NAN. AYA. CAT. BEE.
Seemed only a Moses basket away
when an alphabet of milk
gathered at her lips
and the world was measured in small scoops

Now her little finger is willing
horizons to come closer.
Dance to her wand of utterance.
And in the cave of her mouth
she is rainmaker and sybil in one –
toddler and trickster entongued
by the enchanting newness of noun.

For a Piano Lost in the Lewes Flood: October 2000

(for Serena and her piano)

Not an amphibian
but a creature of land.

Natural habitat:
drawing room
school hall
concert stage
pub corner
where it waits
to be stroked.

Responds to
a child's one-fingered
virtuoso chopsticks.
A maestro's
measured frenzy.
A mother's singing
in the dusk.
Someone's sudden
appassionato
into the past.

Not a creature
equipped for
rising water
and a river's
ever widening hands.
Not a creature
meant to squat
in a river's crescendo.

No, a creature
rooted to land
on upright legs,
though in a movie
they moved one
down the Amazon.
But this is real life
in a Sussex town,
and this is the river Ouse
drawing on its ancient source,
and this is my friend
Serena's grand piano –
a victim at the altar
of the element
that consumes
as it cleanses.

A Man from the Far Right Is Having a Nightmare

His sleep is in a state of vertigo.
He's being pursued by a piano.
One of those grand concert hall affairs
intended for a maestro
is after him
        up the stairs
        down the stairs
        but where are the stairs
        and why do they lead nowhere?
His legs can't compete with legs of rosewood
or for that matter mahogany
and what's that tinkling in his blood?
Looks like there's no escaping
        those integrated ivories
        that snap at his heels
        and seem to mock
        his mobility.
Those rows of black and white teeth
grinning all their sharps and flats
mistaking his tossing and turning for middle C.
If only he could regain submission
to a peaceful pentatonic sleep.
Enough of this harmonic progression
screams the man from the Far Right.
Thank God for alarm clocks and daylight
that restore black to black and white to white.

Grand Ole Piano Mama

I'm a grand ole piano mama
as grand as grand can be.
Touch my ivories, and I gets hot,
I love it when you tinkle my spot.

I'm a grand ole piano mama
as upright as they come.
But stroke my keys like you mean it
and I just might try lying down.

I'm a grand ole piano mama
Insides of steel, yet sweet of tone.
Eighty-eight teeth, and all my own.
Tonight, I'm in the mood for flesh and bone

Reception

Welcome to the Dark
at the Top of the Stairs.

The five-star hotel that caters
to your deepest fears.

Make yourself at home
among the ghoulies and gnomes.

They might be invisible
but O so approachable.

Already the table's laid
and your bed's been made.

Under spiderweb curtains
you can have a lie-in.

Room service is a scream away.
Brought to you by a bogey tray.

Try the chef's creepy-crawly pasta
served in a bowl of alabaster.

If you wish a wake-up call,
just ask the shadows on the wall.

White Actor Prepares To Be Othello

Watch me summon darkness
to my thespian chest.
Why not dare to be black
and get my agent off my back?
My King Lear brought madness
to such sweet perfection,
not a dry eye in the house.
Audiences saw their stalwart cheeks
turn loose with sorrow.
But that Moor, how manifest that Moor
when I strut Stratford's boards?
Shall I invoke the muse of melanin?
Perhaps root out my family tree
for traces of darker kin?
What if I inject a street-cred note
with some hiphop in my stride
to modernise his Moorish pride?
Ah, Max Factor to the rescue.
Mahogany, my instant hue.
We're halfway there.
I smell catharsis in the air.
Yes, I shall blacken my face
and be quite beautiful.
A relaxed lion.
I'll tread the thin line of race.
Inhale his story.
Lose myself in the folly
of skin.
A white handkerchief, my nemesis.

In Times of Peace

That finger – index to be exact –
so used to a trigger's warmth,
how will it begin to deal with skin
that threatens only to embrace?

Those feet, so at home in heavy boots
and stepping over bodies –
how will they cope with a bubble bath
when foam is all there is for ambush?

And what of hearts in times of peace?
Will war-worn hearts grow sluggish
like Valentine roses wilting
without the adrenaline of a bullet's blood-rush?

When the dust of peace has settled on a nation,
how will human arms handle the death of weapons?
And what of ears, are ears so tuned to sirens
that the closing of wings causes a tremor?

As for eyes, are eyes ready for the soft dance
of a butterfly's bootless invasion?

Starting Somewhere

(inspired by a line from Karen Armstrong's Twelve Steps to a Compassionate Life*)*

Nearly every day there is something to forgive –

the tiny stone
that brought discomfort to your heel
the forward frost
that dared to carpet your windscreen.

Nearly every day there is something to forgive –

the fallen leaf
behind your own untimely fall
the bastard fly
that chose to swim in your cereal.

Nearly every day there is something to forgive –

the spilt coffee
that makes a beeline for your dress
the train that limps
just when you're overlate and overstressed.

Nearly every day there is something to forgive –

Something tiny.
Something quite unremarkable.
Something at the time unforgivable.

Maybe if we set our sights not too high.
Begin say with the bothersome stone
or the intrusive fly

Then maybe –just maybe – we'll forgive flesh and bone.

Nine Months in the Life of a Dictator

Before he grew
into a brooding statue
overlooking a nation

a scan once caught him
sucking his thumb
in the womb's aquarium.

His arms were little fins
and his mum needed no word
to feel a miracle brewing.

Like any average foetus,
he was swimming flower,
flesh and bone petal.

Water was his applause –
an umbilical cord
his winding pedestal.

The Executioner

The slump of a hanging form
has the precision of a dance,
the principles of symmetry,
the stillness of a photograph.

That is why the executioner
likes to see himself as an artist.
Execution, like any art,
requires practice, dedication.

Much as the pianist surrenders
to the tyranny of scales,
the executioner puts in hours
to ensure the final perfection.

Maestro of the condemned,
he rises to silence's anthem.
For him no ovation compares
to the radiant climax of the rope.

At the end of a day he returns
to his passion for roses
and garlands his wife's neck
with a rosary of kisses.

Sloth

From his bed of cosmic slumber,
my father, the god of procrastination,
sent me into the world as messenger,
saying: 'Go, but take your time, son,
for your name shall be Sloth –
the one who celebrates indolent growth.'

So I descended aeon by aeon by aeon
with my message of no-rush-to-do-anything.
I breathed my turtle breath over sleeping
form of man and woman
by way of initiation into the take-it-easy clan
that they may learn to take things as they come
and loll in the arms of procrastination.
Then people walked at dawdling pace with face aglow,
for nothing was so urgent it couldn't wait until tomorrow.
And all was good and laid back as the grass.

But the days, the years, the centuries passed,
and soon frenzy took hold of the new breed.
They sang in praise of the go-getters.
Raised monuments to the jet-setters.
Forgot the slow diligence of chrysalis and seed
for all was judged by the cult of the instant
that made a sudden god of speed.
I remember saying to my old mate Morpheus:
Poor mortals. It's all go. Hellbent rollercoaster rush.
How can they manage without the likes of us?
Morpheus nodded agreement before nodding off,
putting his shoulders to the wheel of sleep.

Disguised as a tramp, I sat beneath city walls,
mumbled incantations outside subway stations
and scribbled graffiti to the speeding nations.
SLOTH IS THE MOTHER OF INSPIRATION.
INSTANT FIRE. INSTANT ASH.
But who would heed an old man's limping scrawl?
They sang in praise of the iPad go-getters.
Raised monuments to smart phone jet-setters.

Still I sing in praise of all you loafers
who make the sofa your enduring altar.
Blessed be all you philosophical couch Platos,
limbs enshrined in the turtle's repose.
Viva my votive reclining unwinders
who watch quarterly bills grow into final reminders.
All ardour to your pursuit of languor.
Long may you subvert the tyranny of stress
with inert ways and daring indolence.
For the star of sloth shall rise
again above the frenzied.
Restore the art of crossing one bridge at a time.
Teach the slow gospel of grass and seed.
But not today. Maybe tomorrow.

Unmaking the World in Seven Days

Unmaking the world in seven days
will take some doing. Not a job for amateurs.
Start by remoulding six billion souls to original clay
and the merest relic of a rib –
which by the way takes a while to master,
despite bullets, bombs and natural disasters.

On the second day, let the sky's dominion
be out of bounds to winged fowl
and consign the great whales to oblivion.
Insist that the waters call a halt
to all that bringing forth
of moving creatures after their kind.

On the third day, say good riddance, stars,
you've done your bit for signs and seasons.
Let there be no discrimination
between the greater light and the lesser light.
Keep things nice and simple.
No dividing the day from the night.

On the fourth day, you've got your work cut out.
All that grass must go. Far too much green.
The same goes for busybody herbs and trees.
About time they stopped all that yielding of seed
and return to uncluttered void. Nothingness.
Earth without form is potential bliss.

On the fifth day, you'll be up to your neck
in a formless firmament of waters
and possibly by now a nervous wreck.
But stick with the job of unmaking the world.
Think of a firmament as a demolition job
and you'll be laughing. The tricks of the trade.

On the sixth day, unmaking is a piece of cake.
It's a case of returning earth to the beginning,
restoring the map of formlessness,
accepting the voice of the deep,
saying, let there be dark and there was dark,
as you watch the light go back to sleep.

On the seventh day, you face your hardest test:
How do you, having undone a miracle,
pat yourself on the back and take a rest?
Yes, when you survey your unmaking spectacle,
how do you say, Behold, it was very good
without an audience of leaf, beast, stone, blood?

The Hosanna of Small Mercies

Blink of green to greet the day.
What more can one ask of a leaf?

Blessing of a bird's octaves.
What more can one ask of a beak?

Breath of morning's first coffee.
What more can one ask of a bean?

Embrace of musk from old books.
What more can one ask of a shelf?

The hosanna of small mercies.
The salutation of self to self.

Enemy

Pause to wonder at your enemy's mouth
which, like yours, also boasts a tongue –
that little reptile that blossoms
into the gift of speech and song.

Investigate the ruffle of seaweed
that is your enemy's hair –
a clump not unlike your own.
And one nose per person seems only fair.

How familiar are your enemy's fingers –
a crablike entreaty that could pass for prayer.
Marvel too at those toes – ten, no more no less.
See how they barnacle an instep.

Observe, if you dare, your enemy's eyes,
how they wrinkle their petals –
eyes that, like yours, have smiled and wept
long grounded in the skull's coral.

Ask yourself what's to be done
with this creature, part flower, part sea,
daring to be loved as much as yourself.
This miraculous mirror called enemy.

The Private Whispers of Trees

If we could eavesdrop
on your private whispers, Trees,
what news would we hear you tell
from the depths of your green?

See how the snail keeps
your secrets in its cave of shell –
going nowhere in no hurry.
Little sibyl whose lips are sealed.

See how the bee browses
the weathered braille of your bark,
but reveals the honey of your text
only to an audience of the dead.

And those birds that make
your branches their troubadour perch,
they announce the day but don't let on
what your roots confide in a sleeve of earth.

Must human bones become your bed
before your silent syllables are read?

Under the Cloak

Time to go under the cloak
there where you unburden the workaday yoke
and feel your acorn heart grow into oak

Time to go under the cloak
there where you converse with ones who screech and croak
and prophecy takes on the wings of a joke

Time to go under the cloak
there where darkness anoints your lips with bardic balm
and I am loses itself in I Am.

Ancestry

Coal
born in womb of earth
you whose black heart burns bright –
you the eye of the hearth –
dark bulb glowing in the mouth
of night.

Chalk
born in bed of sea
you dweller in fossil-white-
keeper of these Albion hills –
you from whose rib flint
takes flight.

Slate
born of mudstone and water
you the blood of both worlds –
metamorphic child of clay,
you whose silver-grey veins
yield light.

How Do You Get to the New Jerusalem?

Walk on, stranger, through England's pleasant pastures
till you come to what's called a dual carriageway.
Mind how you cross, stranger, traffic can be dodgy.
Especially with them Satanic lorries.

Look out for a pub called the Lamb of God.
They do brilliant chips with mushy peas and cod.
But things have changed. Not like in ancient time
when on Friday nights the bards battled in rhyme.

Now you'll meet pilgrims of the Happy Hour
whose burning gold is a chalice of lager.
Now a Quiz provides a bit of mental flight
and the till ticks over on a Curry Night.

And while taxis are hailed for chariots of fire,
tribal rage is known to mingle with desire.
But should you meet a heart that sings love's anthem,
then my friend, you've found your New Jerusalem.

Travel Light Travel Dark

Travel light. Travel dark.
A seed in the earth.
A baby in the womb.

Travel light. Travel dark.
Blood through the veins.
Sap through a leaf.

Travel light. Travel dark.
A star in a cloud.
A shell in the sea.

And so a hermit's bowl
becomes a globe

and a walking stick
a sundial.